Mov

by

Clarissa Gosling

Published by Prinsenhof Publications

2019

Text Copyright © 2019 Clarissa Gosling

Cover Copyright © 2019 Steger Productions Design

All rights reserved.

To my husband for bringing me on this adventure with you

PART ONE: Intro

Our story

At eight months pregnant with our second child I came to the Netherlands for the first time. We visited the place that had offered my husband a permanent job, and explored areas where we might want to live if we were to take up the job offer. After we returned he accepted that job the same day I went into hospital to be induced for her birth.

Four months later the four of us came here on holiday to scope out places to live. We ended up finding a house which we would buy on that trip. Then we moved from the United Kingdom to the Netherlands when she was eight months old, and our son was nearly three years old. I am now writing the book I wished I'd had to help me organise our move, to help guide other families who are making an international move.

For us, because of the length of the notice period for my husband's previous job, we had a long lead time for our move. That meant that we had time to organise everything, which was a blessing with a new baby and a toddler. We sold our house in the UK and agreed to buy one in the Netherlands. We sorted through all of our belongings and got rid of lots, before we packed it all up and had it shipped here. We had time to research different places to live and work out what was important to us. And we could do things to say goodbye to our old house and to create mementos of our move.

I know that for many that isn't the case, and you're expected to jump up and move with maybe only a few weeks' notice. I hope that this book will help you with the things you need to consider when looking for a new place to live, and all the things you need to make your move successful.

I will try to make this book as relevant as possible to all countries, while including examples from our experience and from friends. While all countries have their own details and quirks, I hope that I can give some guidance on what to look for in your own situation.

Our situation was a move from the UK to the Netherlands, which isn't all that far for an international move. But we still left all of our family and friends behind to start anew in a place with a different language; a language none of us spoke before we moved here. We are lucky to be close enough we can still go back to visit a few times a year, and that friends and family come frequently to visit. In fact, having space to put up visitors was one of the key things we looked for in our house.

We are just approaching the five-year anniversary of our move here. Both children are happy at the local Dutch school, operating mostly in Dutch with no problems. We are part of the community and celebrate the local events, as well as keeping up some British traditions too. I worked hard to learn Dutch and have got a Dutch as a second language qualification. My husband is also taking lessons and working to improve his Dutch. His workplace is mostly English-speaking, so that limits his ability to practise. We are pleased with the town we have moved to and (at the moment anyway) have no plans to return to the UK.

Who this book is for

I am writing this book for families who are also planning to move abroad. For those who aren't sure what to do and how it would work. While it is based on our experience, I aim to make all the advice applicable whichever country you are moving to.

If you're moving within the military, or diplomatic service, this may not be so relevant as generally you would be moving to join a group of fellow nationals already in the country. So many of these issues will be no problem, or already organised for you. And while this book may be of some interest for those families planning to tour the world and/or world school their children, it is really aimed at those moving to one specific place to settle there for a length of time.

While your new work may provide you with support, and possibly the services of a relocation agency, this book covers topics wider than they are likely to do. I hope that this book can help you figure out which issues are important to you and what you will need help with.

Moving with children gives you different priorities, whatever their age. You need to find schools or childcare and learn how a new education system works. You need to entertain them and find out what there is to do where you now live. And critically, they need to make friends as well.

Every family has different circumstances and different priorities, so will make different choices. The important thing is to make them purposefully and with consideration. This book should raise some issues you need to think about, and give you some questions to help you decide what is best for your situation.

Is your main priority for your children to go to the best school in the area, or for you to afford to have a certain size house and garden, or for you to have lots of activities and events on your doorstep, or something else? Understanding the answer to this question for your family situation before you first plan the details of your move will help you cut down the options and find the best solution for you.

This book is partly the story of our experiences and partly a more generalised set of pointers for you to think about when planning your own move. The book is split into three parts, the first of which is an introduction. This gives you an overview of our story and goes into more detail about what this book does and doesn't cover.

The second part looks at what you need to think about before you move and what you can do to help plan it. The third part looks at what you need to do when you first arrive, when you're settling in over the next few weeks and months, and a few longer term considerations. Lastly, there is a conclusion and overview of the book.

What this book isn't

Please note that this book isn't a specific checklist of what to do in order to move country with your family successfully. It should give you ideas of what to think about. I hope that it will reassure you and encourage you to move abroad. But I will not cover details on everything, as that is far too complicated for one book. Also, that would need to be done for every possible pair of countries to be comprehensive and that would be far too much.

Two subjects I will only touch on lightly are education and languages. Anyone moving abroad with children will need to put them into school and that is important to get right. But every country has its own school system and so I can't provide all the specifics. For more details you must find out what the system is like at your destination of choice.

If you are interested in finding out more about sending children to the local community school, then I have another book on that subject. It is called "Raising bilingual children: when school speaks a different language" and it should be available from the same retailers as this one.

In no way should this book be considered as legal advice. I touch on legal issues, but with a very broad brush and based on my own personal experience not any legal background. If you need advice on your specific situation, you should consult a lawyer specialising in the laws of your countries relevant to you.

PART TWO: Before you move

Overview

Moving to another country is quite a daunting prospect, especially when you're doing it with children in tow. When you move somewhere else things are always different. Even moving in the same country the differences from where you'd been before can be striking. Add in a language difference and food differences and it can be overwhelming. This section will cover all the things you need to think about before you move: employment opportunities, things to consider when choosing a place to live, and some practicalities with moving.

Chapter 1: Opportunities

Before you can start planning to move abroad, you need to have an idea where you're moving to. And while it is possible to move to anywhere in the world there are different restrictions depending on where you're moving to and where you're coming from. I will split this section into moves within the EU, and then wider.

I will also take a quick overview of some differences when moving for employment, or as a self-employed person, and what you should consider if you're an accompanying partner. This will only be an overview of some issues surrounding these questions, and points for you to research further, as the details of all these possibilities are beyond this book.

Within the EU

Within the European Union (EU) all EU citizens have the right to freedom of movement. This means that there are no restrictions on EU citizens moving to, living in, and working in other EU countries. There should be no discrimination based on country of origin for being offered a job, or for how much someone is paid to do that job. This is a right enshrined in the Treaty of Rome, which is one of the original treaties founding the EU. The freedom of movement of goods, services, labour and capital are the underpinning values of the EU and are at the core of everything else it does.

What this doesn't give you is the right to go and live in another EU country only to take advantage of their social security and welfare provisions. It is a right to freedom of movement for labour - so people who are working. Dependents are included within this right, but not anyone wider than that.

One of the major changes happening at the moment within the EU is that the United Kingdom (UK) is in the process of leaving the EU. Quite how they will manage it is unclear at the moment, but it looks like these four freedoms of movement are not going to continue to be applied between the UK and the EU.

Exactly what the consequences will be are still to be confirmed, but assuming it actually goes ahead, UK citizens will lose their citizenship of the EU and so will be unable to move so freely within the EU. Also EU citizens will be under different rules for moving to the UK. For those British citizens (like us) who are already making use of the EU's freedom of movement and are resident in a different EU country, it looks like because of Brexit we will lose the right to move to another EU country.

So if we wanted to move from where we currently live (the Netherlands) to another EU country (for example France or Spain) we would need to go through their process for immigration the same way as any other person from outside the EU. Hopefully this situation will become clearer over the next few months.

Beyond the EU

When we look wider than moving within the EU, there are a lot more things to think about and different permutations of what needs to be done. The entire world is open to you, yet you need to consider the practicalities. Many countries have strict requirements for who can move there and get a work permit. You need to be sure you meet the criteria for wherever you're moving to. Also research the standard length of time to get visas and work permits approved for you and any other family members that will need them.

There are specific treaties between some pairs or groups of countries to facilitate the movement of people. For example, I know a few Americans who have moved here to the Netherlands under the Dutch American Friendship Treaty (DAFT). So check if there is a similar treaty between the two countries relevant to your move.

You should also think about language. Moving to somewhere where you already speak the language makes it easier, whether this is the official language of the country or the de facto language of where you would be living. Though even if the countries speak different languages, if they use the same alphabet that can make it easier for you to learn the new language.

Even in places that share a language there are often differences in different places. The culture shock between the USA and the UK is huge, even though they both speak English.

I can't forget the first time I went to the supermarket in the United States and looked for milk. What was a perfectly ordinary thing to everyone else there was mind-blowing to me. I had no idea what fat percentage was equivalent to the semi-skimmed milk I used back in the UK, and what about all the things that had added to it? Calcium and Vitamin D - was that something I wanted, or not? And the bottles they came in were so much bigger than I was used to.

More things to think about when considering which country you want to move to are what type of religious/ government structure are you happy with? Do you want to move to a developed country, or a more developing one? Also think about any health considerations relevant to your family. For example, living at altitude or in high levels of pollution might not be possible for someone with asthma. Do you need to access particular health equipment/ treatment/medication and is that available where you're thinking of moving to? Do you want to move closer to locations where you can practise a particular sport, i.e. skiing or surfing?

What about the climate differences and environment? For example, would you be happy eg in the Middle East where you might not have very much time outside because of the heat? Or would you be ok living in China with high levels of smog in the cities for much of the year? What about weather? Do you want to move somewhere that has better weather than where you currently live? What about seasonality? If you've always lived near the equator, then it can be more difficult to acclimatise to somewhere that has differing lengths of days at different times of the year, and vice versa.

Obviously for some people the area they live in will be dictated by the type of job they're looking at, like finance, academic research. For others there will be a much wider range of possible locations to choose from.

Another consideration wherever you go is how do your qualifications match with those in that country. Would you be able to start work straight away, or would you need to pass another set of exams? Would you need your certificates authorised or verified? Your employer should be able to help with this. Alternatively, contact the issuing body for your qualification, or the professional body where you're moving to, as they may be able to advise you.

Employed v self-employed

When looking to move abroad for work it's important to research the criteria the country you wish to move to has for allowing people to work there. Some countries have limits on who can migrate, points systems for deciding who is eligible to come, and requirements for visas and work eligibility, while others have schemes to reward highly skilled migrants with tax breaks and the like. Check the details of who can immigrate and whether you are eligible for any of these benefits.

If you are accepting a job offer, then talk to their HR department, as they should be able to advise you on these details. Especially in larger corporations they will have a lot of experience dealing with these rules.

If you are taking up a new job abroad, then you should also be aware of how secure your contract is, and what criteria there are for any probationary period. It is a lot of upheaval to move abroad and then if it all goes wrong you could end up stuck. Think about possible back-up plans and what you might do if the worst happens.

Now, most of this discussion so far has assumed that you are moving to another country where you have received a job offer. You can also move as a self-employed person, though I believe that the rules are stricter and you have to prove your income. Check what you'll need for the country you're planning to move to. Many countries have this information available online so you should be able to find it. Or at least contact details to ask for them.

If you are moving when self-employed then you must investigate whether the regulations covering your job are the same, and whether your qualifications are still valid. You should also research what market there is for your skills, and how easy it will be for you to pursue your line of work with little language skills (assuming that's the case). Alternatively, there may be a niche market you can develop, for example English-speaking plumbers might be high in demand in an area where there are lots of English-speaking expats.

Another consideration is your tools - will you be able to use the same ones, or does your new country work to different standards? How easy it is for you to transport them all, or will it be easier to buy new when you arrive? There are no right answers to this, as it will depend on your individual situation.

Whether you are employed or self-employed, it is never too early to investigate your pension. Especially when you are moving between countries you need to think about how all of your pensions accumulate and how they can transfer. What pension rights does your new position have? What social pension rights do you have in your new country? And what do you still have a right to from your previous country? Do they offer reciprocal rights or the opportunity to transfer? Can you make contributions either in your home country or the adopted country if you're not working and when do these kick in? I discuss this further in the section on Retirement.

Accompanying partner

If you're moving as a family you need to consider the accompanying partner, or trailing spouse. This is the adult who hasn't got the job offer abroad, so is accompanying or trailing after their partner. They have to decide whether to transfer their work too (if they're able to), to stay at home, or to move and search for a job there. There are pros and cons for each of these decisions, and they all depend on the exact details of their job and how transferable it is.

If their job can transfer and has a local office with a suitable position available for them, then that is the easiest solution. You will need to set up childcare before you move, so that both of you can go straight to work. If they want to search for work once they've moved then you will need to find out what visas they need. Also, investigate how easy it is to get a job there without knowing the language (assuming that's the case). If they want to stay at home, then you must find a support group, as staying at home all day every day is hard.

In our situation this was me, as we moved to the Netherlands for my husband's work. When I first became pregnant with our second child, we decided that I would take a career break, to stay at home with the children. So when he was then offered the job it was easy for me to agree to stay at home in the Netherlands, rather than in the UK. For us, this made the decision to move easier.

An important consideration that not many people consider before moving is what happens if, once you've moved, your relationship breaks down and you want to split up. There are significant issues, especially around child custody and moving internationally. Many countries are signatories of the UN Convention of Children's Rights and the Hague Convention on the Civil aspects of International Child Abduction.

This means that if the relationship breaks down your divorce and custody proceedings will probably be done under the law of the country you live in, rather than where you're from, and will take those two pieces of international legislation into account.

Depending on the age of your children, how long you have lived abroad, and what you plans were for how long you would stay, your new home is likely to be considered the habitual residence of your children. Which likely means that the assumption will be they should remain in that country. This has additional implications for an accompanying partner, as if your ex-partner is the only one of you with the security of a good job, they may automatically get custody.

So you might be forced to choose between staying in that country, where you may feel alone and unsupported with job prospects that might not be as good as where you're from, in order to stay near your children, or moving back to your home country, friends and family in order to resume your career but forced to leave your children behind. This is a heartbreaking choice.

When you're working out the details of your split, you will need to discuss custody and country of residence of the children, and also permission for holidays. Your ex-partner will need to give you approval in writing every time you wish to take your children out of the country, for example, to visit your family, otherwise you could be accused of child abduction. If you are caught taking them abroad without your ex-partner's agreement then you could end up in prison, or with your rights to see your children severely restricted.

On the flip side you have to give permission for your partner to travel internationally with your children too. This is not something that is often flagged to families before they move and can make the already difficult process of divorce even worse.

Airports and international travel agencies have the right to ask parents travelling alone with children for proof that the other parent approves of the trip, and can stop you travelling if you can't do so. Even if you haven't split up know that as an adult travelling alone with children you can be stopped and asked, so you should always travel with copies of your partner's passport and written confirmation they agree to the trip, with details of where you're going and for how long.

It's better to have them with you and not need them, than to have your travel plans disrupted while the border agencies track down your partner to check that they are happy about your trip with the children. Both my husband and I have been asked where the other parent was when taking the children abroad alone. Don't assume that it won't happen to you.

Obviously you shouldn't assume the worst will happen, but being aware of the likelihood will mean it's less of a shock at an already difficult time. Now, this is not a reason not to move abroad, but is definitely worth thinking about and discussing before you decide. In the rage of a relationship breakdown it is easy for one partner to use these restrictions as a weapon against the other, forgetting it's always the children in the middle who get hurt the most.

I would advise you to sit down with your partner while you're still planning the move and to talk through your options if everything goes wrong. Come up with a plan before you need it, so you have a framework to build on to ensure that everyone is considered without so much emotion. It was something I made sure we did before we agreed to move. Then you can move safe in the knowledge you have a plan if the worst does come to pass in your relationship.

Chapter 2: Planning where to live

So, you've decided to move abroad with your family and have chosen which country you're moving to. What next?

There are several key things you need to think about when considering where you will live. If your children are school age, you need to find a school for them in the area. And you need to look at the practical side of where you're employed and your journey to work. It can be overwhelming to try to find all these things in the same area, so we're going to go through some points to think about for all of these questions.

First thoughts

When looking for somewhere to live you need to consider all the activities you will do regularly. How far do you want to live from where you work? Where are the closest shops and supermarket? What are the different neighbourhoods like? What are the school catchment areas? Are there places available at daycare or after school care? What about out-of-school activities? Are there other families from your home country living locally?

Now for a house, you need to consider your budget and whether you want to buy or rent a property. How long you're planning to stay in the area bears on this, as it is often more hassle than it's worth to buy a property if you will only live there for a few years before you move again.

Your employer will no doubt have given you an indication of what salary you will receive, and you can find out from other people in the area what the likely living costs are. Look for indicative costs for taxes, bills, fuel costs, healthcare, etc to work out what your likely monthly costs will be. Or you can look at one of the many online cost-of-living comparisons that rate different cities against each other too. This will then give you an idea of how much you can afford for your mortgage or rent.

It is worth doing your research to find out what the processes are for both renting and buying, as these vary around the globe. In the Netherlands renting is seen as a much more permanent solution than it is in the UK, so renters have a lot more rights to the property they live in.

On the flip side properties here are mostly rented without flooring, light fittings or curtains, as those are the responsibility of the people moving in. Depending on where you're moving to, you might find that most houses for rent or buy are advertised online. This makes it much easier to find something suitable even when you're not in the area.

If you're moving with a large international company, they are likely to be able to help you with finding somewhere to live, so ask what they have available to support you. There are also companies that provide temporary hotel-like accommodation for those moving to an area, especially in big cities. So see what's available online.

One of the best ways to find out about different areas in a town is to visit and talk to people who already live there before you move. If that's not possible you can find out lots of information online. Search for Facebook groups of parents in your area, or other social media. Or see if other people moving to the area have blogged about their experiences.

If you're planning to purchase a house, then you need to look into the requirements for a mortgage. Can you use your previous pay slips to prove income for a mortgage, or can you only apply once your employer has paid you in the new country? Are there any other ways to prove your income that the bank will accept? What is the process for agreeing a rental or purchase? What are the timescales? At what point does it become legally binding? What are the penalties if you break the agreement? These are all points that change from country to country, so I will not go into detail here as I don't know where you're moving to.

Be aware that as someone who doesn't know the system, you are a target for unscrupulous individuals who might try to scam you. Do your due diligence and make sure you're not being overcharged for being a foreigner. Find someone who you can trust to help you. If you've found a local group online, then that is a good place to look for recommendations, as well as things to look out for in the process, and to get an idea of what is normal.

What about other activities you plan to do regularly? Are you planning to have a car, or to rely on public transport? Do you need a garage or parking space? How close to school and/or daycare do you want to live and work? How far are you willing to travel to get groceries or to go shopping for clothes?

List all the places you will need to go to and make life easy for yourself if you can. An important factor when considering how you will get around is the cost of fuel, so work out how much it is likely to cost you to run a car and make your normal trips.

Also consider finding somewhere temporarily for when you first move, as then you can find somewhere more permanent when you know the area better. The downside of this is that you must move twice and possibly have to keep your things in storage for a while.

Children

Of course, if you're moving as a family then you have to consider what the children need. Depending on their age daycare or school is the big one. And if you are both going to be starting work soon after you move, then you need to get places for the children organised as soon as you can.

You will also probably have a legal requirement for school-age children to attend school in your new country of residence. This deadline may mean that you are forced to choose wherever there is space left, so I would advise you to start looking as soon as you have an idea where you will move to.

Finding schools, daycares and/or after school care that are all convenient for where you live and work is the key. But it can be a jigsaw puzzle where you have to choose one in order to get the others agreed. Schools can be wary of offering you a place until you have an address, and you don't want to commit to a house until you know there is a place at a nearby school. There's a longer discussion about choosing schools and daycares in the chapter on settling in.

Another thing to investigate when looking for a place to live is outside space. Where is your closest playground or park? Depending on where you choose to live and what it's like you may have limited garden space of your own, so look for communal or community spaces.

While having your own garden is nice, and it feels more secure to let the children play there on their own, they are a lot of work to maintain. You need to weigh the benefits up for your family. And in urban areas larger gardens are increasingly expensive, so find out what alternatives there are. This can be more difficult to find online as not all areas list what facilities they have.

Walking the streets is the easiest way to find what's local to you, and to see where the local children play, but that's difficult to do if you're not in the area. If you can visit and have a look round, then keep an eye out for children playing in the road, areas covered in sidewalk chalk, signs asking drivers to slow for children, or any other sign that other children live in the neighbourhood. Walking round at different times of the day can give you a good feel for a neighbourhood too.

If you're not able to visit the town and wander round, then Google Street View can help, if the place you're interested in is covered, though be aware that those images may be out of date. And it takes almost as long to look along every street using that as it would to walk round it.

Alternatively, you can look on a map and find the green spaces, though those are often only the larger parks, not necessarily all the local play areas. If you can find a tourist map of the region, they often mark local sights and places to visit and if you're lucky, it might mark the smaller play areas too.

Going further afield it's worth looking into nature organisations, historic monuments, museums, urban farms, zoos, theme parks, and other attractions to see what else there is to do in the region. Depending on where you're planning to move to there will be different opportunities. Many of these now do annual tickets so if they're nearby you can visit frequently and always have something to do.

Here in the Netherlands for example, there is an annual ticket for all museums in the country, which we find well worth having. Most of the museums have activities for children, and as you haven't paid entry, you don't feel so tied to staying there all day and getting your money's worth. This means if the children get bored after a few hours you can do something else without feeling guilty. Having an idea of what there is to do in the wider region where you're planning to move to really helps you to be prepared for after you have moved, when you want to start exploring. We're still working through our list of places to visit nearby!

Work

This brings us back to work and balancing that with where you want to live. Think about the balance between travel time/costs and how much house you can get for your money. Only you can decide how far from your work you are happy to live. How long a commute are you happy with? What are the public transport links? How is the rush-hour traffic?

Most people live a distance away from where they work, so end up travelling backwards and forwards between the two. Work out how long a journey you are happy with and be realistic about what the travel times really are in peak hours.

Look at trains and buses too. Consider the travel times, frequency, and the travel costs. Some employers offer interest-free loans for season tickets, or there might be a tax advantage for using public transport, so enquire about that with your HR department.

Could you cycle, or run to work? That has the advantage of keeping you fit and healthy without having to fit another activity into your schedule. Check what bike storage facilities there are at your work, and where the showers are.

And think about splitting up the journey. For example, my husband cycles to work one day and then cycles home the following day, travelling by train in the other directions. Or you could cycle to the train, or bus stop, and leave your bike there.

Depending on your job, are you likely to have frequent trips away? So how easy is it to get to the airport, or international trains? How much does this need to be factored into your choice of location? Also, how are you, as a family, likely to be travelling? Are you going to be flying frequently? The ease of getting to the airport on your own is different to doing that with children and multiple items of luggage in tow.

Final choice

All of this should help you come up with an area where you'd like to live that meets all your requirements for how you want to live. Combine that with your budget and you can look for what's available. Do you want to live somewhere for a short time, while you get used to the country and get to know the area, or do you want to move as few times as possible?

Once you've narrowed down your area of interest, you must look for what houses are available. Some employers can help with this, and may even have houses they can provide to you. If not, then maybe they can recommend someone who can help you. Some employers can provide temporary accommodation for when you first move. The longer you have before you start work, the more likely it is that you will find exactly the house you're looking for.

Estate agents are a good contact as they can advise you what's available in an area and they may be able to tell you about properties before they come on the open market. Here in the Netherlands there are separate estate agents for the buyers and the sellers. A purchasing estate agent can help find properties and negotiate with the sellers on price. They can also advise you through the process, as this differs in every country, and on who else can help.

We found our purchasing estate agent invaluable in our move as they made it all so easy. And he specialised in doing everything in English, so he translated all the documents. He also put us in contact with a mortgage broker who dealt in English too. He even arranged for a small amount of building work to be done at the house before we moved in.

While the process will probably differ where you're moving to, finding someone on the ground who can talk your language and guide you through the process makes it so much easier. You will also need to ask how much any deposit will be. As you might need to pay up to six months rent as a deposit, and/or fees to whatever broker found your property for you. It is better to find out how much the bill is likely to be before you need to pay it.

Chapter 3: Practicalities

Once you've chosen where you will live then it's important to get the practicalities sorted. In this chapter we will look at some general points about the process of preparing to move, look at utilities, what to do with all your things and any pets, and discuss transport options. If you are working with a relocation agency, then they may do much of this for you. Even so, it's important to understand what they're doing.

Preparing to move

Once you've decided to move, you need to tell people you will be leaving. The exact timing of when you tell different people is up to you and depends on your situation. You may want to involve parents/ grandparents/ siblings/ friends in the process, or only tell them when it's all decided.

The other big question is when do you tell the children about the move? This depends on their age, the certainty of your destination and the timeframe it will likely happen in. You know your children best. But in most cases the more you can involve them in the discussion the easier it is for them. If you can visit where you'll be moving to then they will visualise it better. Though the younger they are the more difficult the concept of time is, so they will struggle to understand what's going on.

If you're moving to a country which speaks a different language, then it is a good idea for the whole family to start learning some of the language. That way it won't be so much of a shock when you first get there. How much the children will be able to learn depends on how old they are.

Once you've found somewhere to live, the next thing to do is to plan your actual move. How will you get there? Will you fly, drive, or go by public transport? These take different lengths of time and allow you to bring different amounts of things with you. Later in the chapter we will look at what you do with the bulk of your possessions and any pets you may have, both of which will have a bearing on how you plan to move.

If you own a property in your home country, you will need to decide whether to rent it out or to sell it. Both have implications for costs and time needed to organise and get it done. Especially in the UK selling a property is a very fraught process. We were lucky we were already trying to sell our house before my husband was offered the job, so all that changed was we made sure everyone knew that we had a definite date when we would leave. The sale wouldn't happen sooner than that, but equally it wouldn't happen later than that. And we did successfully sell the property on that day.

If you have a much shorter time frame before you move then you may not be able to complete this process. You may need to ask someone else to manage the sale or rental of your previous home. This could be a friend or family member, or you could use an estate agent to do it for you.

For the actual move you may want to find somewhere temporary to stay for the first few nights while you sort your furniture out. Depending on what time the removals arrive, or if you need to find new furniture once you arrive, you don't want to have tired children and no beds ready for them to sleep in. This also gives you a base away from the chaos of boxes, and stuff to do, so you can relax. We booked a room at the local hotel for the first two nights after our move here to the Netherlands, which made it much easier with a baby and a toddler as we knew there was somewhere they could sleep.

Depending on your employers there may be some flexibility in start dates and finish dates, which you can use to give you some time to get everything sorted in your new house before you start work. Are you going to be able to have some time in between jobs to move and settle into your new house and area?

If you can give yourself a gap between the date you plan to move and when you start work, that gives you some breathing space. If you have annual leave from your previous employer, then you can use that to create a gap in which to move, so that there's not so much of a gap between paychecks. Then you can explore as a family and find out where things are and what there is to do. Obviously how much of a gap you can have depends on finances and the exact details of your arrangements with both employers.

If you can unpack and put away most of your things before you go back to work it helps mentally. It means that the whole burden of sorting out all of your possessions doesn't fall on your partner, or get left so you live amongst boxes. It can easily take over your evenings and weekends when you'd rather be doing something else - like exploring your new place of residence.

Administration

Admin is a boring topic, but important. Create a file of your most important documents in a safe place (birth certificates, marriage certificate, passports, health records, vaccination records etc). You may need to get these translated or apostilled in order for them to be valid in your new country, so find out what you will need so you have it ready when you need it. I discuss this further in the section on when you first arrive.

You need to cancel and close accounts with all your providers for your old place of residence and set them up for your new one. The first thing to do is to make a list of all the things you need to give notice on in your old house. Think about things like water, gas, electricity, cable, satellite, internet, mobile phones, landlines, insurances, etc. Also look at any memberships of gyms, automobile associations, community groups, local attractions, loyalty cards, etc. These can have different notice periods, so check as you don't want to be continuing to pay for things you can no longer use after you've moved. Mobile phone contracts especially can be a pain with a long notice period.

Once you've moved, you will need to work out what you need to set up again for your new house. Bizarrely the tricky one for us to set up was electricity and gas. For some reason our online application didn't work, and when I called them to do it over the phone they insisted on doing the whole conversation in Dutch, as apparently any legal contract has to be done in Dutch. So somewhere the power company has a recording of me just blindly agreeing to everything, as after only a couple of months living here my Dutch wasn't good enough for me to follow what they said. But we got power!

We found car insurance was also difficult, as we (to start with) drove our UK car to the Netherlands. Our UK insurer wouldn't cover us for a non-UK address, while Dutch insurers wouldn't register a UK car. In the end we persuaded a Dutch insurer to cover us with our UK car, but it involved a long international phone call and the agreement that either we would sell the car within six months, or legally import it and register in in the Netherlands, which was our plan anyway. Once we'd moved in and settled we decided we didn't need a car so we sold it without replacing it. The section on personal transport will discuss importing cars and considerations related to that.

You should look into whether your driving licence is valid in your new place of residence. You may need to get an international driving licence, or take the driving test where you now live. For us, as EU citizens in the Netherlands we could just swap our driving license for a Dutch one easily, although now with Brexit it will probably be more difficult. Driving rules vary round the world so it is worth reading up on what they are in your locality before you do too much driving.

Like any other house move there will be a myriad of address changes. You may be able to set up a post forwarding service to your new address, though setting that up internationally can be expensive and, depending on where you're moving to, may be very delayed before it reaches you. Alternatively, you can set it up to forward to a trusted friend or family member who is hap-

MOVING ABROAD WITH CHILDREN

py to sort through it for you. Over time, you can update all the addresses, so this is a task that diminishes.

You also need to deregister with any healthcare provider (family doctor, dentist, etc) so they know not to keep you on their books. You should be able to get a copy of your notes to pass onto your new healthcare providers, which will make the transition easier, especially if you have any ongoing medical issues. Be aware that you may need to pay for the admin time of collating your notes in a format for you to take with you. When we moved my file from our family doctor was over a hundred A4 pages long for ten years with that practice. That's what comes with having given birth twice!

Your belongings

Now we come to all of your things. How much of what you own are you planning to take with you? There are several things to take into account here, for example, how long are you planning to be away? Do you plan to come back? How much stuff do you have? How far are you moving? Some employment contracts include the cost of some removals in the offer, so check what's included and what you can do with that. Is the property you're moving to furnished or not?

Here in the Netherlands it is common for even rental properties to not only be unfurnished but also to have no flooring, no kitchen and no light-fittings. The assumption is that the renter would want to make it their home and choose their own. Obviously if you're moving internationally, having to fit out your house in an unknown place is a daunting prospect. For this reason, a temporary solution may be a good option for you at first.

Moving house is always a good opportunity to reassess what you have, even more so when it is a long-distance move. Depending on how much notice you have of your move, will affect how much time you have to go through your things. We had seven months' notice, because of my husband's notice period at his previous employer. However, we also agreed to move the same day I went into hospital to give birth to our daughter, so we needed that long period of time to cope with both changes to our family life.

Also, as our move wasn't far, on the scale of international moves, and we had a budget for removals included in my husband's job offer, we brought pretty much everything with us. We had a bit of a clear out, and got rid of some stuff, but the vast majority of what we owned came with us.

You don't have to move all your things with you. Especially if you're moving a longer distance, and if you're planning to move back after a few years, you could choose to take only your essentials with you, put the rest in storage, and buy what you need new once you've moved. This is also a good option your furniture is in a certain style which might not fit the house you would move to.

Not bringing everything gives you the opportunity to clear out all those things hiding at the back of cupboards you've never really liked. Then you need only replace the items you require. If you're moving to a place with an established ex-pat community, then you can often find people who are leaving and selling all of their things, so you don't need to buy everything new again.

Also consider bed size standards. Different places have different standards of bedding formats, which mean your bed linen won't fit properly. So it's easier to either bring all your bedding with you, or buy it all new, rather than mix and match. We brought all of our UK sized bedding with us, and are now, bed by bed, changing over to European sizes when we need to buy new. But it makes washing and changing sheets more complicated as I have to keep separate all the different sizes and keep track of which goes on which bed.

Another thing to consider is your electrical items. Not all countries use the same electrical supply standard, and therefore electrical devices may not work properly where you are moving to. Transformers are expensive and inefficient, so it might be easier to buy new rather than transport your old equipment. Where the electrical supply is the same, but the plug standard is different, you can easily get plug adaptors.

A good idea where you will have multiple items with old plugs in the same place is to use multi-socket adaptors, as then you only need to have one adaptor plug. These are also helpful for guests when they come to visit. For the first few months after we moved we kept buying more plug adaptors as we had underestimated how many we needed, so bring more than you think you will need.

Also look at what food you have in the cupboards and freezer, so you can try to eat as much of it as possible before you move. Some countries, Australia in particular, have very strict rules about bringing foodstuffs into their country and you need to be very careful that you comply with this. Even if you're not moving somewhere as strict it's still easier not to be transporting large amounts of food with you, especially food that is easily obtainable where you're going.

Before we moved, we had some fairly random meals, eating up what was in the freezer, and we gave away some things too. There were some that came with us though, mainly things you only use little of, like the mustard powder we still have!

Also look at your drinks cabinet. Do you still have a half bottle of Limoncello from a holiday to Italy five years ago and are you really going to drink it? What alcoholic beverages you can take with you also depends on where you're moving to. Some countries are dry, and you could be at risk of heavy fines if you take alcohol into them without a license. I know of people who have had a cocktail party before leaving to drink up all the random bottles of alcohol they weren't going to transport.

When you've worked out what you're bringing, you can then plan how to move it, either to take with you, to put in storage, or to get rid of it completely. Organising removals, either to your new house or to a storage facility, will need to be booked in advance.

You may not be able to time the delivery of your belongings at the same time as you arrive, in which case you will need to take with you what you're likely to need to tide you through until they arrive. Remember to include favourite cuddly toys, books and games for the children. Also take all of your valuables and important documentation with you, rather than including them in any removals.

You are likely to want to take a certain amount of money with you too. You will need cash to start with to cover your living expenses until you start earning, to pay a deposit for the purchase or rent of a house, and to pay for anything you need to buy when you first move. This means you need to exchange currency to what is used in your new place of living.

There are a range of different options for this, and obviously it depends on how much you are taking with you. You can use your local bank, a specialist currency exchange firm, or increasingly there are online options too. Check the fees and rates associated with each of them, and the speed of when the money will be available to you.

Pets

Pets can be an incredibly emotional issue, whether you leave them behind or take them with you. With the use of pet passports the possibility of taking your pets with you is becoming easier.

The decision to bring your pet or not will depend on what pet you have and their age, where you're going and what the rules are for bringing animals into that country. Depending on what type of pet you have you must check if they are allowed where you're moving to, as some breeds of dog and wild animals have restrictions on them.

If you want to fly with your pet, then you must check the rules and regulations for the airline in which you're travelling and the rules for transporting animals in the country you are leaving and the one you are going to. You may need to have your pet microchipped, purchase a special travelling cage, or have specific vaccination documentation. It is worth finding these out with plenty of time before you move so you can get these in place. For some destinations you can't take animals on the plane with you and they have to be shipped in a specialist freight plane.

If your pet is old, then you may not want to stress them with a long journey, possibly in a plane, and then settling in to a new place to live. Here it might be kinder to re-home them, maybe with a local friend so you can still come back and visit them.

As kids my family was given a cat by neighbours who moved abroad, as he was old and not expected to last much longer.

If you're planning to leave your pet behind, then you will need to prepare your children for this, so they can get used to the idea that their beloved pet will not come with them. It's a good idea for you next time you're back in the country to come and visit. Then everyone can see the pet thriving in their new home.

On the other hand, if you're taking your pet with you then you also must have a plan in place for making your pet feel at home once you reach the other end. Do they have a special blanket or bed you can take with you, or have them travel with. Or certain favourite toys they can keep with them. Once you move, you must help them settle in, which may mean keeping them confined to a few rooms until they get used to being there, or taking them out frequently to walk round and explore the area. Depending on what sort of pet you have you will know what's best for them.

If you're staying somewhere temporarily for a few days while you get your house sorted you may need to think about how you handle that with your pet, as they may not be able to stay with you. Depending on the distance you're moving you may be able to leave your pet with a neighbour for a week or so. Then come back to pick him up and bring him to the new house once you're more settled in, although that will not work for all situations.

Personal transport

Once you've moved, how do you plan to get around? I would definitely advise you to think carefully about whether you need a car. If you already have one you want to import, look at how much that costs and what the process is. Compare it to the cost of buying a new car when you arrive. What sort of car do you need? Will you be using it to commute? Are you going to use it mainly for long trips and weekends away, or day-to-day popping round town? How much luggage are you likely to carry in it? Will you need to take the whole football team to matches every Saturday? Or just for the weekly grocery shop? What other options are there?

Does your house have allocated parking or a garage? If it doesn't how close are you to suitable parking spaces, and how busy are they? How easy is it to get a parking permit for your work, if you're planning to drive there? What does it cost to park at different locations you are likely to visit and are there enough spaces to go round?

Petrol costs and running costs vary in different regions. If you're importing your car what checks and registrations do you need to do? Are there annual checks to make sure that your vehicle is road-worthy? How much do they cost and where can you get that done? Finding a local reliable garage is important, so you have somewhere you trust to look after your car when it has a problem. Once you've moved, you can ask your new neighbours for advice. Alternatively, look for reviews of local garages online.

Look at the public transport links where you will live. Where are your closest bus stops, or train stations? Where do they go to? If you've made a list of local attractions, then look into ways to visit these by public transport. Some places give you money off the entry cost if you come by public transport or bike.

Then look at what's in walking distance, or what you could cycle to. If children are brought up being active, walking and cycling to get to places, then it becomes a habit and helps keep them fit. Maybe I'm biased living in the Netherlands, where there are more bikes than people, but cycling is such a common occurrence here. Small children sit on extra seats on their parents' bikes and bigger children cycle themselves. In fact, I have difficulty stopping my youngest, who is five, from taking her own bike everywhere.

Don't rush this decision, in fact you don't have to make it before you move. It is a good plan to know of what options there are available to you and then consider them in more detail once you've settled into your new home.

PART THREE: After you've moved
Overview

In this section I will cover settling in to your new country when you first move, both the official things you probably have to do and also what you can do to start feeling at home there. Next, we'll look at some wider issues, like getting to know people, combining cultures and hosting visitors. I have a whole chapter dedicated to healthcare, as this is important to set up correctly before you need it. Lastly, there is a chapter on longer-term issues like learning the language, becoming a permanent resident, voting and retiring in your new home.

Chapter 4: settling in

Now you've moved. You've got an almost empty house, or one full of cardboard boxes. It's time to get everything set up for your new house and explore the neighbourhood. This chapter looks at some legal and official things you will probably need to do when you arrive in a new country, exploring the shops and amenities in your new neighbourhood, choosing schools, daycare and/or after school care for your children, and creating a weekly schedule for yourself.

When you first arrive

There are always legal/official details you need to deal with when you first arrive. Do you have to register with the town hall or the police? Should you register with your home consulate in the country where you're now resident? If so, what documentation do you need to do this? Your new employer will probably be able to advise you, as they also want you to be correctly registered in order to be legally employed.

Most countries, even within the EU, require you to register with the town hall or police when you move there, as they maintain a record of who lives where. As a Brit this was not what I was used to, but it wasn't a problem. We needed to take our birth certificates and marriage certificate and we were registered and received our registration numbers. We could then use these to get a bank account, health insurance, register with a doctor and all the other things we needed to do.

We didn't need to translate our documents, but we needed to get apostilles for them. This is an official stamp to confirm that they are true copies of the national birth and marriage registers. For this we needed to order new copies of the documents (so that they were produced within the last six months I think) and that service also offered an option to apostille them. We could do this easily online and they were sent to us ready to take into the town hall. We originally registered with just our English copies, as we didn't realise we needed them to be apostilled, and then took the apostilled ones to the town hall a month or so later when we had them.

The format of birth and marriage certificates across the world varies, and the officials in your new place of residence won't know what to look for in these documents from any other country. So you get them apostilled by your country as a proof they are genuine. An apostille is issued by your home country (or wherever the document was issued by) and is then internationally recognised.

Do you need to get a social security, or National ID number? How do you go about doing that? If you're not sure then asking your new employer is a good place to start. If they often bring in staff from abroad, then they will be able to help you through the process and know exactly what you need to do. Alternatively, there might be organisations that exist solely to support new immigrants through this process.

In Amsterdam we went to what's now called the IN Amsterdam Centre who helped us register and get set up with the paperwork we needed. They also gave us a helpful booklet on "Your First Month in Amsterdam", which had lots of useful tips and checklists. If you can find out what you need to do, and ideally make appointments to do this before you move, then it makes it much easier.

Once you've got somewhere to live with your belongings in it, it's important to make sure you're properly insured. Buildings insurance, contents insurance, car insurance, travel insurance, legal insurance, health insurance, there are a myriad of types you might need.

Is there a comparison website for insurance in your new country? In the UK there's moneysupermarket amongst others, in the Netherlands there's independer.nl. I'm sure that similar sites exist in most well-developed countries. These sites will advertise to people looking for insurance, so they'll probably rank highly if you search online for insurance and the name of your country.

Alternatively, you might be able to get deals on insurance through your new employer. In the United States, for example, health insurance is often part of any employment package. We'll look at healthcare and insurance in more detail in the chapter on Healthcare, as there are lots of related things to think about and it's important.

You will also need to open a bank account, so find out what you need to do that. International regulations on money laundering require you to show proof of identity, but you may also need a national tax identification number, or social security number. In that case you may need to wait until your local registration has been processed before you can open your bank account.

Be aware you will need to have enough cash available to cover all your expenses until you are up and running. In some places you won't be able to access your bank account until you're paid into it for the first time. Many jobs pay in arrears, so you start work and can work for up to a month before your first paycheck arrives. Add to that any time you have between moving and starting work and you could need a substantial sum of money to keep you going for a couple of months.

Depending on the country you're moving to, credit cards and foreign bank cards might not be widely accepted. Some otherwise very wealthy and highly developed countries operate essentially on a cash economy. It can be a shock to discover that your credit card is not valid at the supermarket when you go to buy groceries.

And of course you need to unpack and sort out the house. It's a good idea to get the children's rooms ready first to help them settle in to their new place. Then work out what you need to purchase and what the priorities are. Some of this you will have worked out when you decided what you were bringing with you or not. For example, we knew that we needed to buy a washing machine as soon as we arrived. With a family of four, and two of them using cloth nappies at the time, we ran a load of washing most days. And so we couldn't be too long without one.

On a more mundane level it's important to find out when and how your rubbish is collected. Is there a communal place to put it out, or do you have kerbside collection? Personally I still feel an immense sense of achievement whenever I put the rubbish out on the right day. But then we have four different wheelie bins that are collected on three different days of the week on a weekly, fortnightly, three-weekly or monthly schedule.

Shops & amenities

Once you've got the paperwork sorted out, or maybe before you do, you'll need to find some food. I find supermarkets are strangely disconcerting places to visit in other countries. Each country has their own logic for where to find different things. In France you have the giant hypermarkets which sell you everything you might ever need and take about a week to walk round. At the other end of the scale, here in the Netherlands most supermarkets aren't much bigger than any other store, and most people shop multiple times a week.

I love going round supermarkets, wherever I am, and just looking at all the different things and how they're organised. As I said before, here in the Netherlands supermarkets are smaller, with a lot more Indonesian food available, compared to what I was used to in the UK, and less Chinese and Indian ingredients. The reason for that is the historical spread of the respective empires and trading blocks. We have been enjoying learning about this new range of foods and cooking more schnitzels and mashed potato dishes than I used to in the UK.

One tip I would give you is to take your time when shopping, though I know this is much easier said than done especially with small children in tow. Consider going out alone, later in the evening after the children are in bed, to have a detailed look around your local grocery store. Don't try to do too much in one go to start with.

The Google translate app is handy - it can even overlay the translation on the camera feed, which I think is amazing and really comes into its own in a supermarket when you're not sure what something is.

While it's nice to wander round the aisles discovering new foods, it can also be stressful when you can't find what you need. Especially if you have small children in tow who want to be somewhere else. When we first moved, and the children were small, I tried to make sure I had a short list, and so went shopping more frequently, and I tried to make sure there were only a few items on my list I knew I would have to search for. In this way I could limit the time going back-and-forth round and round the shop.

Eventually I learnt where most things are, but it took me a few years to do that. If my husband goes shopping, I still give him directions for where to find things I'm not sure he'll find on his own.

Not all supermarkets are the same, they often vary in price. So it's worth having a look round after a couple of weeks or so to find out if there are different options for where to shop. Which chains are cheaper, or which chains have more of the things you like? Is there an out-of-town shopping centre? Also look for independent shops: butchers, fishmongers, greengrocers, bakers, etc, as they may have better quality food to sell and be able to advise you on how to use it. Look for a local market, as that might be worth a visit.

My children love going to the smaller shops and the market as they are invariably given a bread roll, a slice of ham, a banana etc to eat while I'm ordering what I want. Now they're both at school it's become a holiday treat to come with me to the market!

Once you're a bit more settled, experiment and try out new foods. Look for free recipe cards in the supermarkets, or packet mixes. Try local restaurants or takeaways. Choose a new favourite food from your new home. For me the Dutch apple tart takes some beating, and we also enjoy the odd Indonesian take-away. I admit I haven't yet got up enough courage to cook Indonesian food myself though!

Make a list before you move of what large items you will need to purchase once you arrive. Do you need a washing machine, fridge, freezer, dryer? Any furniture? Plan what order you must get them in and think about how long it may take for these to be delivered.

A washing machine will be a fairly high priority if there's not one already where you're living, especially with small children who get through clothes at an alarming rate. If you've found a local group, then they will be a good source for where's the best place to buy these, or for finding a laundromat if you need one in the meantime.

Once you've found the basics, then look further afield. What are the shops like in the town centre? Are there any out-of-town shopping areas? I got stuck on where to buy things like a baby changing mat, or a landline phone. We found them in the end, but had to ask the neighbours as we had no idea which shops sold those and I hadn't seen any on my shopping trips. Each time that there's something new that you haven't bought before you need to consider where you might find it for sale.

As you get used to what's available in your new locality, you can think about whether there are any favourite food items from home that aren't available in your new home. If there's a particular brand of toiletries you like to use, where can you find it? Or will you need to have visitors bring it when they come?

We have a list of things we ask people to bring, and while the list is getting smaller over the years, there are some things we will continue to import. Marmite, proper English tea, custard powder, brown sauce, golden syrup, treacle, Cadbury's chocolate and big blocks of cheddar cheese are all on our list of things to buy in the UK. While some of those are available here in the Netherlands they're often smaller packaging or not quite the same, so we keep our stocks from the UK as a little bit of home here.

After a while there are likely to be things you want done and you're not able to do yourself. This could be finding a good hairdresser, a cleaner to come regularly, a plumber to fix the toilet when it leaks, or a myriad of other jobs. With many of these you can easily search online, look for adverts in the local paper, or find a business based closed to where you live. But a personal recommendation is best, so ask neighbours or in local online groups for who they would advise you to go to.

Especially with children, it is important to mix days of unpacking and doing chores, with days of going out and doing things together. So take your list of places to visit and choose where to go first. Depending on the time of the year there will be a variety of things to see and do, whether it's just going for a picnic in a nearby park, or heading out for a day at the zoo.

Show them, and yourselves, the benefits of your new location. Investigate all the great things you can do. Go for a trip to nearby towns to explore and see what you can find. Take a bus or train trip just to enjoy the ride, you might even spot something interesting or helpful out of the window on the way. Smaller children love doing this - there doesn't even need to be a reason to go anywhere, as the travel can be enough to entertain them.

You don't even need to travel - we've spent mornings sitting at the train station waving at the drivers, without going anywhere else!

Childcare & schools

If you both have jobs lined up to start soon after you arrive then you may need to have childcare and/or schools organised before you move. If not, then you will probably have a little more time in which to work out what you need and to get it arranged. Depending on where you're moving and how busy these places are you might find that many of them have waiting lists, and you're unable to start straight away. In which case you will have less choice over who looks after your child than you might have wished.

Look into all of your options - if you have smaller children then, as well as daycares, see if there are child-minders in the area. These often have a smaller number of children and look after them in their own home. This can make it easier to leave small children as it feels more homely, although it may be more difficult to find when you first move to an area.

See if there is a national register of childcare options - many countries require anyone who does this to be registered and monitored regularly. This will give you an idea of quality and may also include feedback from other parents as part of the report. You will probably need to translate this, as it's unlikely to be available in multiple languages.

School starting ages differ round the world, so it's worth finding out about how the school system works in the country you're moving to. It surprised us to find out (after we'd moved) that school in the Netherlands started at age 4, literally the day after the child's birthday.

We moved a few months before our eldest's third birthday and hadn't given a thought to looking at schools, or taking that into account, when we were looking for our house. Fortunately, there was space at the local school and both children are now very happy there, but that was completely down to luck.

Many countries make their education inspection reports available online, so you can see how they are rated according to their criteria. Of course these may not be translated into a language you can read. Google Translate is good to give you an idea of what something says, but it is not perfect. I wouldn't advise relying on it for anything important, but you can use it to get an idea of what the report says. Always visit in person to get a feel for the place yourself if you can. If you've found a local Facebook group, or similar, then ask for recommendations. Or search the group to see if anyone else has asked about the places you're interested in.

Finding a school place can be tricky, especially if there is an application process for children in anticipation of the start of school, either primary or secondary. If you arrive between that happening and the school year starting it might be difficult to find somewhere. The best thing is to talk to any schools as early as possible, maybe even before you have a house sorted, if you are worried. They will be able to advise you on the process and what you need to do.

Be aware that you might need to have multiple children at different schools, or start at a second choice school and then have an option to change later once places are available. Keep in contact with the schools and your children about what's going on. The less time you have to arrange school places the less likely it is that you will be able to have your ideal solution, but you can make the best of it.

Depending on the age of your children and where you are moving to, they may need to attend a language school. This is a special school for helping newcomers to learn the new language, before they go into a normal school. This helps them to not be kept behind because they don't understand the language rather than the subject matter.

For older children this is more important as they are developing more complex ideas at school, which can be hampered by not having the language skills. It is perfectly possible for children to be thrown into the top years of school in a different language and excel. So if a newcomers' language class isn't available then it doesn't mean you automatically have to choose an international school, if there's one available in your language.

You just have to understand that you and your child will have to work harder to keep up with their classmates. In any case it's imperative for you to maintain close links with the school to help them support your child.

Once you've got your school place organised then, if you need after school care as well, talk to them about what options there are for this. Depending on how the day is structured, you may need to arrange care over lunchtime, as some schools still expect children to go home for lunch. The school will have a system in place and a list of providers that serve other children in the school, as you won't be the only family who needs this service.

Overall, just try to relax about this process. It can be very stressful, especially when you're looking for places and there feels like nowhere for your child to go. At the least in most developed countries there is a requirement for children to attend school.

This means once you register your school-age child as being resident there the municipality has an obligation to find a place for you. Though that won't always be in the location you would prefer, but as I've said, it may be possible to move once you've started, if a place elsewhere becomes available later. You will then need to weigh up the upheaval of changing school and friends and routines against the improvement in the schools.

Every country has its own school system - when children start school, how many types of school there are, how they progress through the years, when they finish school and what that can lead on to. It is worth doing some investigating so you have a basic idea, especially about whatever bit of the system your child is in.

Norms and assumptions can be wildly different, so try to approach it with an open mind. Just because it is different to how you're used to doesn't mean that it's better or worse. It's just different. Every system has its good and bad points. If you're interested to find out more about how to help your child when they go to the local school in a different language then look out for my book on "Raising bilingual children: when school speaks a different language".

As well as local schools there are often international schools, British schools, French schools, German schools, American schools, etc and fee paying options. These are generally more expensive, and often full of expat children where school fees are part of the package offered to their parents to move there.

If your child is nearing the end of their school career, you could also look into them remaining in your home country, either at a boarding school or staying with friends or family, and visiting you during the school holidays. You may need to make someone a legal guardian for your child if you do this, so they can make decisions about your child on your behalf. If these might be something you want to do, then you will need to look into the costs and feasibility for your situation.

Depending on the country moved to/ from there may also be an implication for university entrance and fees if the student hasn't been living in the country in the years prior to starting study.

Another option to look into is home-schooling. This is not always easy to get approval to do though as different countries have different laws. If you're interested in doing this, then try to find other parents who can advise you on the process. For example, here in the Netherlands it is very rare, and once your child is registered for school, then you have almost no chance of getting agreement for home-schooling.

Whereas in the UK it is much easier to get approval and there is a growing community of home-schooling families across the country.

When looking at the costs of these different options also consider if you can get tax back, or childcare support. These can help, as childcare is often very expensive. When you move, you may be eligible for child benefit from your new country, but you will need to find out what the rules are, as it's different for every country. Then if your children will go to daycare or after-school care then there may be a system for tax rebates to help with the cost of that.

In the UK you could pay money towards childcare from your salary before it was taxed, so that was money you received without paying tax on. Here in the Netherlands you can get a proportion of your childcare costs back, depending on the salary and weekly hours worked for you and your partner.

To find out more about how this works in the country you're moving to you must ask someone. The HR department of your new employer should be able to help, or see if the local tax office website is available in multiple languages.

The rules for who needs to submit an annual tax return, when the deadline to do it is, and what you need to include varies between countries. You may also still need to submit a tax return in the country you have moved from. If you are an American citizen then you will have to continue submitting a US tax return every year for as long as you remain a citizen. Even if you have no economic tie with the country anymore.

If you feel you need someone to guide you through the process, then ask for recommendations for a tax adviser or accountant. Neighbours, colleagues, or contacts in local social media groups will be able to give you names of people who can help. If it needs to be done in the local language, then it is especially helpful to have someone do it on your behalf.

Schedule

Once you have got over the novelty of moving, and have started getting things sorted, the next hurdle is when work or school starts. If you're at home with the children while your partner goes to work for the first time then plan what you will do. I think I took the children to a local play area that has a cafe on my husband's first day.

If you can get out of the house, purely so you don't feel trapped in it. As I discuss in the section on mental health, it is important to look after yourself, and spending time outdoors can be key for that.

I found it helpful to have a weekly schedule of activities to guide me through the week, especially at the beginning. This is especially useful if you're the one not working and have children at home with you. Even if you have nothing organised create a plan, preferably where you get out of the house every day. It can be something as simple as: Monday we go grocery shopping; Tuesday we visit the Library, Wednesday we go to the park, Thursday we go to the train station, Friday we go to a cafe for a drink.

Having a schedule means you have an idea every day of something you will do. And you can then amend it, or fit other activities round that. Or invite other people along with you, though not necessarily to grocery shopping!

Having a plan gives you a focus for the day and getting outside is important for your mental health and increases your chances to meet other people and form connections. Don't stay trapped inside the house.

If you have to do school runs, or have any other activities, classes or groups scheduled then those make a good start to setting up a weekly schedule. Is your child still young enough to need naps, and if so how many? Does your child sleep better at home, or out and about? Do you need to make sure your child gets a run-around? Do you need to include a rest period for you both? Take these into account to make your plan work for you.

As well as school or daycare you'll want to look for activities and groups. Are your children currently doing a sport, or activity, that you'd like them to continue with? Do you want to find a baby group, so you can meet other mums? Or to find activities for you? Then look for what's available in your area and take these into account when choosing exactly where to live. Libraries are often good places to see a range of different activities, or any local community centre.

As most groups now have an online presence, it is easier to find out what's available than it was a generation ago. However, be aware that scheduling different activities for multiple children and ensuring everyone has dinner and gets to bed on time can be a logistical challenge, but it's worth it. Then as time goes by you change this schedule to fit the changing activities and growing children.

When working out what activities your child will do, you must consider the balance of those between what you're familiar with language and culture wise, and what is new. When you first move you don't want to overwhelm them, and yet full immersion is the best way to learn. And once you've been there a while you'll want to support their home identity and language too. So if you can find activities with people from your home country it helps, especially in the early days when everything is overwhelmingly foreign.

If you have moved to a country where they speak a different language then you need to consider how well your children have picked that up before they start activities on their own in the community language. For us, our children were young enough that they had a good grasp of Dutch before they did things on their own. And as nearly everyone speaks English to some level, it is easy for them to ask for a translation if they don't understand. But I realise that this isn't always the case.

Personally I joined a local orchestra fairly early in our stay here. I wanted to do something for me, rather than always being an appendage of the children. As I'd always played music, I looked for a local group to join. They were friendly, though at the beginning it was tricky because I still didn't know Dutch that well. When we were playing, I followed the conductor's instructions as best as I could, though to be honest I ignored whatever I didn't understand, and I got on fine. Chatting to the other players was difficult for a long time, but I attempted to speak Dutch and they appreciated that. I am still a member, and in fact I was recently voted onto the committee.

Chapter 5: Looking forward

You've survived your first few weeks or months. You know where most things are and you have a sense of the area you've moved to. Now it's time to look forward in order to work towards making this place your home. Do not underestimate the emotional side of moving away from everyone you know and into a foreign place. It can be disorientating and feel wrong at the start, but over time you will find things you love about it, and become part of the community.

In this chapter we will look at meeting people and making friends, staying in touch with people from home, some tips for travelling, as you're likely to be doing that more than before, and the fusion of cultural traditions.

Meeting people

Making friends can be for many the most daunting part of the whole process of moving abroad, especially when you speak a different language. If you're working out of the house, then you have colleagues and co-workers as an automatic group of people you interact with.

For those who are not working, or working from home, this can be the make or break aspect of any move abroad. It takes a while to find a group of people, so in the beginning it will be lonely. Reach out to your neighbours and other parents you meet. Be proactive at chatting, or asking people to come for coffee. I know for many this can be difficult, but it beats being alone all the time.

I have gone up to strangers in playgrounds and say "Hi, I heard you speaking English. I'm Clari. Here's my phone number. Let's meet up and have coffee sometime." Suddenly your language becomes a point of commonality. And likely they are also feeling a lack of their usual support networks and are more than happy to get to know someone new.

I am shy and find social chitchat difficult with most people even in English and harder in Dutch. But I made myself talk to people so I wasn't spending all my time with only the children. Now I have a group of close friends and a wider circle of acquaintances. That takes time to develop, so don't despair in the beginning. And I still force myself to be the one who makes contact with the new parents at school, and to join in with conversations rather than sitting on my own.

If there are opportunities to help at school, then that can be a great way to get more involved with more people. Do they have events which need volunteers to help run, or can you join the parent-teacher organisation or become a governor? For younger children schools are often looking for people who can come in and read to them, but that depends on how good your language skills are. Helping at school also helps you get to know the teachers and be in the classroom so you can see how your children interact with their peers. This also helps you pick up on any problems sooner than you might otherwise.

Then after school has started, or before it ends, if there's a few parents from my kids' classes hanging about in the schoolyard I join them. It's good to keep up with what's going on and helps get to know them. The smaller your children are the easier I think it is to meet people. Once they're old enough to go to school alone, then you lose out that interaction with other parents at the school gate, or in parent and child groups.

If you're working, and unable to be at the school gate, then ask other parents if there is a class chat group to keep up with what's going on at school. Local Facebook, or other social media groups, can be helpful to provide you with contacts nearby, as can going to local events and meeting the families of your children's friends there.

Libraries and local community centres are good places to look for activities where you can meet people. With the influx of immigrants into many western countries there are more and more activities organised for them, so you may be able to join in with those. These could be language or integration classes, games sessions, story sessions for children, arts and crafts activities, bring and share meals, or help with doing your taxes. You never know what there is until you look.

Sports clubs or music groups can also be ways to get out and be sociable. Consider taking up something new, or picking up something you've previously done. Learning the local language helps with getting to know local parents and neighbours, and language classes can be another place to meet new people. I'll talk more about different options for language learning in a later chapter.

Depending on what language you speak at home, you may find a local ex-pat group for your nationality. Or to find a more general group for ex-pats of all nationalities. Sites like Facebook, Meet-up, Yahoo groups etc can all be good places to look for these groups. And social media is great for keeping in touch with all your friends back at home.

Getting to know other people can be the most difficult part of the settling-in process, and it is one of the most important. It requires you to be proactive - to go out and try to connect with people. Just making eye contact and smiling can be enough to break the ice, as they are probably not going to come to you uninvited.

If they are all in well-established cliques, it can be even harder to find a way in, but there will be other people outside those groups who you can make friends with. It will take time and effort, but persevere and you will get there. You may need to step out of your comfort zone, but have faith in yourself that you are worth knowing and can give back. You can never have enough friends!

Friends are important for your children too. If they're in the local school, then they may find this difficult until they have mastered some language. This is likely to be more of an issue the older the children are. Younger children seem more able to overcome any language barriers when playing together. They too will find their tribe in time.

Staying in touch

One of the biggest issues can be that you are far from your family and friends. They aren't round the corner anymore and able to help. Especially with children, the distance and the fact they see each other less can severely impact the bond with grandparents and wider family. Fortunately, there are few places in the world without internet access, so you can now easily talk through VoIP services like Skype.

We have weekly sessions set up with my parents and my parents-in-law to talk to the children. You need to be aware of the time difference though. Even an hour or two can be significant, if it impacts with bedtime or mealtimes. Work out when is a good time to talk to each other and when isn't. Calling people in the middle of the night is not the best way to keep friends.

Technology really helps with the transition, as it can help maintain contact with people back where you've come from, and help you contact people living where you're going before you move. Social media can be a great help, both with staying in touch with your old friends and in finding new ones. It was a lifeline for me when we first moved and I knew hardly anyone here.

Once you've moved abroad you are more likely to have people wanting to come and visit you. Obviously this depends on your exact location, but you may find that you are now a holiday destination. Your new hometown is probably a far more interesting place to visit than wherever you were before, at least in people's perception. Having enough space to be able to host visitors is helpful, or at least knowing where the closest hotel is.

For various reasons we had our first visitors to our new house in the Netherlands within a week of moving. Most of the boxes were still full, and we were nowhere near settled, but it was lovely to see them, and they were happy to pick their way round the boxes. If the same happens to you then be clear on whether you can realistically have them stay in your house. Recommend a nearby hotel if you feel that would be easier for you.

I find having visitors is a great way to get out and explore new things, showing off the area where you live and all there is to do there. Look again at your list of local attractions and see where you haven't been yet. It can be difficult organising trips suitable for everyone though, especially if that includes small children and elderly or disabled people. With thought and planning you can make it work.

Then on the other side of the coin is the need to organise trips back home. With flights being fairly cheap it is easy to visit back again, though it depends how far you are going. You need to think about your finances and what time you have available to work out how often you will realistically be able to go. One benefit of living abroad is being able to explore where you now live, so you don't want to spend every school holiday going back to where you used to live, although it is important to see people there when you can.

When you are planning your trip think about how many people you will be able to see, and who those are. Remember school holidays don't always line up, and people will probably work during the week. So if you're not careful it's easy to end up with weekdays with nearly nothing and then jam packed weekends. The people you left behind will carry on with their own lives, and things will change there too. It can be a shock to discover that it isn't the same as when you left.

Try to balance the amount of driving round and visiting large groups of people with days where you do less, as otherwise is can be overwhelming for the children and you. One thing I try to do when we're visiting people is to be clear about what time we plan to arrive, what time we plan to leave and what food we will need. It can seem rude to say "we'll arrive at 12 can we have lunch straightaway, and then we'll stay til 3," but it makes it so much easier for you and them if everything is clear beforehand.

Children (& husbands) can get very grumpy when they're hungry, so knowing when and where you will get your next meal can be a lifesaver in a day of going from house to house to see different people.

Do you want to have particular rituals or habits you do every time you go 'back' to help the kids stay rooted in the home culture? We often visit the UK over Christmas and for the last few years have taken the children to a pantomime during our visit. I must admit having struggled to explain what they are to Dutch friends after the holidays!

Are there things you need back home that you don't need in the new country, especially if the weather is different? Things like wellies, waterproofs, or winter clothes could be left with someone you frequently visit. Even if you do use them where you now live you can always keep a second set with Granny, then you don't need to transport them backwards and forwards each time. My children love using the bicycles my parents-in-law have and the difference from their bikes is part of the appeal.

Travel

Moving abroad means that in order to visit family you will probably travel more and further than before. This means you need to be happy to travel, which often involves long car journeys or flights. Although obviously the closer you are to your old home, the easier it is to get back there.

Flying with babies and small children can be stressful, but it is important to be prepared. Make your expectations clear to your children, and yourself. Have a system that everyone is clear on and soon your children will get used to how it works and what they need to do.

Have things with you to feed them and to entertain them whatever method of transport you're using. And bring more than you think you need in case everything is delayed. There's nothing worse than being stuck with hungry and bored children. New toys are always appealing, but remember it's difficult to pick things up off the floor in an aeroplane or car, so don't bring something with lots of small bits. And I limit it to colouring pencils when we're travelling, as I think those are easier to get rid of any marks that end up where they shouldn't be. Sticker books are also great.

When travelling by plane stress that in the airport they need to stay with you. That there will be lots of standing around in queues, but emphasise what they can look forward to at the end of the journey. Most airlines let you take a buggy or car seat up to the gate which can make transporting small children round airports easier.

You have to ask your airline when you will get those things back, as sometimes they go into the hold and you need to collect them off the luggage carousel with any other luggage. This means you won't necessarily have them for disembarkation or the walk through the airport to have your passports checked and get to the luggage area. This varies by airline and airport, so double-check for your trip.

We found baby carriers (slings, woven wraps, etc) to be invaluable here as you can carry your baby, or preschooler who won't walk, while still having all your hands free for dealing with suitcases or holding the hands of older children. Also, you don't need to check the sling as it folds up small enough to go into hand luggage on the aeroplane. We did once leave one behind in the overhead compartments and never got it back, so triple check you've got everything before you get off the plane!

For small babies, feeding them during takeoff and landing really helps their ears acclimatise to the changing pressure. The regulations on liquids in your hand luggage are relaxed when flying with a child under the age of two, so take advantage of that to bring a bottle (or two) of milk or water with you. I have a few times given that as my explanation when I've forgotten to take water bottles out of my bag. Now they're both older than two I can't get away with that anymore!

Travelling by car has the benefit you're in control of when you leave and where you stop. On the other hand it's a very confined space to keep children in for an extended period, especially when it's full of luggage too. Again, make your expectations clear about how long the journey should take and how they should behave in the car. For small children potty etiquette is vital, there's little worse than being forced to stop every half hour for a child who says they need a wee, but really are playing with a newfound power to get you to stop the car. If your child suffers from travel sickness in the car, then give them their necessary medication in plenty of time and have spare clothes and sick bags within easy reach just in case.

If you can, time your travel according to your normal schedule to try to keep the kids in their usual routine. Work out what time you'd need to leave home to get to the airport in time, and what time you will probably get to wherever you're travelling to after landing, and choose your flight accordingly.

You will be limited by what times flights are available on the right route, but it is worth taking this into account. I prefer flights that are earlier than I'd like rather than ones that would get us to our destination late. In the mornings, if you're organised, you can get up and out the door quickly. And with a packed breakfast on the way the excitement will keep you going.

Whereas at the end of the day dragging tired grumpy children through an airport is not a task I relish. If your child still naps, and will happily sleep in the car or plane, then bear that in mind when choosing times.

When planning a trip by car remember where you are likely to be when rush hour hits. School holidays also impact traffic and how busy the airport is. If your children aren't yet at school, then take advantage of being able to travel out of season. You'll regret not having done that when you're forced to travel at the same time as everyone else and pay premium prices as well!

Cultural traditions

One of the most alienating, and yet fascinating, things about living abroad are the different traditions. How is Christmas celebrated, if at all? Do they have new celebrations that don't exist where you come from? When are the national holidays, as they are different in every country?

One day in the year that really emphasises that difference for us is the eleventh of November. In the UK this is Remembrance Day - commemorating the end of the First World War (WW1). It is a solemn day of recognition for all the war dead since 1914. Just about everyone wears a paper poppy on their clothes, as the fields of Flanders, where many of the fallen from WW1 lay, were overgrown with poppies after the war had ended. And that has become the British symbol of remembrance.

But here in the Netherlands, they celebrate Liberation Day on the 5th May, to commemorate the day that they were freed from the Nazis at the end of the Second World War. As they were neutral in WW1, it makes sense they don't commemorate it ending in November.

On the eleventh of November, at least in the part of the country where we live, they celebrate St Martin, as it is his Saint's Day. He was a Roman soldier who cut his cloak in half to give to a shivering pauper.

And so the children make paper lamps to hang on the end of a stick, and once it's dark, they go round house-to-house singing and are given sweets. It's a cross between Halloween and traditional carol-singing. Though what the link is between the story of St Martin and the giving out of sweets, I'm uncertain!

The haul of sweets that my children bring back lasts us for the next few months. Quite different to the solemnity of remembering those who gave their lives for our freedom.

One UK celebration my husband misses is Bonfire Night. The fireworks on New Year's Eve/Day just aren't the same! But I get two Mother's Days, as the Dutch celebrate it on the same day as the USA does, rather than when the UK does. And without really meaning for it to happen that way I get cards from the children on both occasions.

It can be difficult for you to find out about some of these, as they are so understood by most other people that there isn't much warning. The first year can be disorientating. If you can find other people who can warn you about things, like the likelihood that children will be at your door expecting sweets, then that really helps.

What living abroad gives you is the opportunity to blend your traditions with those of your new country. You can celebrate the best of both worlds in your own way. Keep what's important to you from your home and add in things from your new home.

It might surprise you that certain traditions you didn't pay much attention to when you were living in your home country suddenly become more important. I have a British friend who never bothered much with pancakes on Shrove Tuesday, for example, but now it's an annual fixture in their family calendar.

Chapter 6: Healthcare

Healthcare is one of those things we don't really think about until we need it. So when moving abroad it is important to find out how it works, because when you need it, it's better to have everything necessary already in place. In this chapter we will look at different types of healthcare, the variety of services available, mental health issues, having a baby while abroad and some issues that arise if you should become long-term sick.

Types of healthcare

The first thing you need to find out is how healthcare is organised. Is it a free national system paid for through taxes, like the National Health Service in the UK, or is there a level of insurance required? Does it include dental care, or is that separate? How do you pay for it?

Health insurance works differently in every country, so research what your options and responsibilities are. Here in the Netherlands it is a legal requirement for everyone to have basic health insurance. What that covers and how much it costs is set by the government and reassessed every year. If you are on a limited income, then you can get some money back in your annual tax return.

Health insurance may be part of your employment package, especially if you're moving to the USA. Even if it's not, your employer may have a deal with a specific health insurance company, so ask if that's the case. Then check what is covered and if there are any limitations on changing them. For example, here in the Netherlands you can only switch your health insurer at the start of a calendar year, unless you're moving into or out of the country in mid-year.

Depending on your health and any chronic illnesses or likely use of health care services, it is worth looking at what the options are and what is covered. Contraceptive can be a big cost and here in the Netherlands it's not included in the basic level of health insurance for people over 21. You need to get a higher level of coverage in order to have that included in your package.

And you may want to get a higher level of coverage in order to be able to choose your hospital in the case you need to use one. Otherwise you (or your family member) may end up in a hospital of your insurance company's choosing, which could be on the other side of the country. Maybe you think it is important that if you were to be hospitalised, you would have a private room, and so are willing to pay more for that to be included.

Do you want to include dental care, or have options for glasses? Again, this is up to you and your family. Look at different insurance companies and see what they offer.

Check what is covered for children. Do you have to pay for them? Are they automatically included in your policy? And for children likely facing braces of some sort to straighten their teeth, check if it includes orthodontics. Here in the Netherlands dental costs for children under eighteen are free, but that doesn't include orthodontics. For some insurance companies I've heard that you need to have had the higher level of insurance to cover orthodontics for a year before you can claim on it. I haven't yet looked into this myself in any detail though, as our children are still too young to need that.

I must admit the health insurance here is something I'm still working out. Fortunately, we have had no major health problems so haven't needed to look into things like hospital choice. The children's health service, family doctor and pharmacy we visit frequently, but not much more than that. So far anyway!

Within the European Economic Area (EEA) and Switzerland residents of one country have the right to access state-provided healthcare during a temporary stay in another EEA country or Switzerland. With an EHIC you are able to get any treatment that is medically necessary before your planned return home on the same basis as a resident of that country. This will be at reduced cost or free of charge.

So if you are a resident within an EEA country and planning to travel, it is worth your while to get an EHIC - they are free and make it much easier if you have a problem abroad within those countries. If the country you've moved to is within the EEA, then check with your health insurance provider how you get one of these cards.

Health services available

Within the healthcare system there are always many parts - acute and emergency care, specialists, family doctors, community support, auxiliary workers, and alternative treatment providers to name a few. How access to each of these is regulated can be different in different places. Is your family doctor the gatekeeper, or can you contact other providers yourself? Or do you see separate doctors for different things? For example, a children's doctor, women's doctor, etc.

One point to remember here is that just because a system is different doesn't mean that it is better or worse than what you're used to. It's easy to assume that what you're used to is the best solution, but every system has been created to care for the people in each area. Some places might insist on annual check-ups for everyone, while others might only do that for certain age groups, or people who fill certain risk criteria.

Often the choice of your family doctor is the key to understanding the system. Having someone who listens to you and takes your concerns seriously is important. Otherwise your whole view of the system can be undermined.

When you first arrive and register with a doctor take time to talk to them about how it works, as that will make it easier when you need it. Just understanding the different ways to make an appointment is reassuring. Also, knowing how they work with colleagues - will you always see the same doctor or could you see anyone of those in your practice? Knowing this in advance makes your expectations clearer.

If you have any repeat prescriptions from your previous doctors, then it is important to let your new doctor know as soon as possible so you don't run out.

As for the children, how does the healthcare system tie in with school? How are babies monitored and given vaccinations? It's common for new babies to be regularly weighed and checked that they're developing properly, so if you move with a baby it's good to get into that system as soon as you can so there's no gap. This is often, but not necessarily separate from the family doctors.

In the UK babies are monitored by health visitors, and in the Netherlands it's the Consultatie Bureau who does a similar thing. And in Germany, children are always seen by a specialist paediatrician, regardless of whether they are healthy or sick.

Not every country has the same vaccination schedule, so there may be differences between that for the country you are moving from and that you're moving to. This may mean that your child will need extra vaccinations to catch up with their peers. Your new family doctor will be able to advise you on that, or point you towards someone who can.

Mental health

Your mental health is important. Look out for each other and take it easy on yourself. If you know you have a tendency to depression or anxiety, then plan for how you can look after yourself if that becomes an issue. Make your new healthcare providers aware, so they can support you how you know you need to be supported, and aren't coming at it new when it becomes a problem.

You know best what works for you. Open communication is the key, so your partner knows when you need more love, affection and support. I found the loneliness came in waves and can be triggered by the most unexpected things. Friends at home can help support you, as can going outside and looking at the sky. As long as it's not too grey and rainy!

Accept that it will be difficult at the beginning, but that it will improve. Make sure you do things just for yourself, things that make you feel good. Cook food that reminds you of home, if that helps. Try new things, if that's what you want.

Children can be the best mood relievers, so join in with their games, the sillier the better. Laughter will help you find the good in where you live. Children also have a different perspective as they are forever seeing the wonder and magic in everything. Take them outside exploring and see what you can find, and how that changes as the months.

Most people like to feel helpful, so ask for help if you need it. Neighbours and other parents will understand that you're on your own and don't have the network they might have. The worst they can say is no. One of my Dutch neighbours only seems to call me when she needs help with something, and I'm glad to help her when I can. I'm pleased to be asked, so I don't mind at all.

If you're the one left at home while your partner works, then a lot of the mental load can easily fall on you. For the house, for the children, for the unpacking, for the settling in, for making the move a success. Don't expect too much from yourself.

Take each day as it comes and limit what you plan to get done, especially if you have children under foot at the same time. Talk to your partner so they take on some of this load, so it doesn't all fall on you. And take breaks; don't feel guilty about taking a day off now and then to do something different.

If you're both working, either away from the house or from home, then you also need to come to an agreement about how you will share responsibility for what needs to be done at home. You need to be realistic about what unpacking and sorting you can do, and how long it will take you. Breaks are also important - don't try to do everything all at once. Take time out to do something as a family, even if there are boxes at home waiting to be unpacked. It takes time to get everything sorted, so don't rush it.

Having a baby

When a family moves abroad, it doesn't mean that their family is complete, so you may move while expecting, or become pregnant while living abroad. If that is the case, that you will need to learn about the process of giving birth in another country.

Different countries have different philosophies towards the birth process. The most fundamental are probably whether there is a bias towards home births or giving birth in the hospital, whether elective caesarians are available, and what pain relief is available during labour.

If you are expecting then it's important to look into what your options are as soon as possible. Your healthcare provider will be able to advise you on what's available in your local area. Many hospitals organise visits so you can look round, so you know where the maternity wards are and what's available there, before you need to go.

Again, check what coverage you have in your health insurance policy. How much after-care is included? Does it cover the cost of a lactation consultant, if you think you will need one? How many scans are included? What tests does it cover, or are there others you must pay for privately? Are parenting classes included? Your midwife may be able to help with information about these and guide you through the process.

There may be a national parenting group that advises and supports new parents. In the UK the National Childbirth Trust organises classes for new parents all over the country, which are also a good opportunity to meet other people who are having a baby nearby at the same time as you, so you have a group to socialise with once they are born.

If you have older children then you will probably need to find someone to look after them while you're giving birth so that your partner can be there for you. This can be one of the most stressful aspects of the whole thing! Don't be shy about asking people to help, even if you haven't known them for long. Other migrants are often sympathetic – some of them have been in the same situation too!

Are other family able to come over and visit for this time? Do you have a neighbour who could help? This is a difficult thing to ask as there will probably be little warning for when you will need them, or for how long they'll be needed for. And it may be in the middle of the night. But don't be afraid - people are mostly more than happy to help. And other parents have all been there before and understand the need for you to have your partner with you during this time. If you can have a couple of people lined up to be waiting for the call, it will give you some security that one of them will be able to help when you need it.

After the birth and your return from hospital you'll need a plan for how to get back into your normal (ish) routine with your new baby. Here in the Netherlands there is a service called kraamzorg, where for the first eight to ten days after the birth someone comes to the house for a few hours to help with the new baby. Both my children were born in the UK, so I have no personal experience of this service.

If you're also working, then you must look at what the maternity leave regulations are where you're living. This differs greatly round the world, both in terms of how long you can be off and how much of your salary you are paid. Some also stipulate how long before the due date you must stop working. Planning to return to work, and when, requires a discussion between you and your partner about finances and how it will work for you as a family.

If you will need your baby to go into childcare, then it is worth talking to providers as soon as you can. When I was pregnant with my first, I applied for a place at the on-site nursery where my husband and I both worked weeks before I told anyone else I was pregnant. As I knew that I wanted my child to go there because it had a good reputation and was the most convenient for us. But I knew it had a limited number of spaces for babies, so I had to act quickly to ensure he could go there.

I went back to work just after his first birthday, so he was on the waiting list there for over eighteen months. If you already have children at a daycare or childminder, then you may have priority there, but start that conversation as soon as you can.

Long-term sickness

One factor few people consider when they move abroad is what they will do if one of them becomes long-term sick. Different countries give different rights to social care or benefits, and the requirements for sick pay from employers are different.

My sister worked in Dubai for a few years, and while she was employed there she had an accident meaning she could no longer work. Her sick pay she received from her Dubai employer was 10% of what she would have received from her previous employer in the UK. Now, for her that reduction didn't make a huge difference as she had no dependents and came back to the UK for her continued recovery. But for those of us with a family, losing an income would have serious consequences.

As discussed earlier your health insurance may have a say in which hospital you are treated at if something happens. If their choice is far away, then it can be difficult to manage combining visits along with maintaining the daily routine for the children. So take into consideration what the possibilities are, though everyone hopes it won't affect them.

Chapter 7: Longer term questions

This brings us to the last chapter: longer term questions. If you're planning to stay in your new country long term, then there are a more things you need to consider. Things like learning the language, whether you're eligible to get permanent residence or become a citizen, what your voting rights are. Looking further into the future than that there are questions about your children leaving home and retirement.

Languages

If you will be staying for any length of time, then it's worth learning at least a bit of the language, even if that's just saying hello, asking for a drink, or where the toilet is. If you will be staying for longer, then you may need to achieve a certain level of proficiency for your visa or residency permit.

Being aware of what level that is and how long you have to do it in gives you the ability to plan how you will achieve that. Again your HR department should be able to help you with information about this. They may also organise lessons for you, especially if you need to learn the language for your job.

There are different options for how you can learn the language - group lessons, evening lessons, intense courses, private lessons, or online tools. Have a look round for what's available where you live and what will fit in with your schedule.

Personally I organised private lessons during the daytime, as then I could take my baby along with me more easily. I had no daycare for her when I started, and by the time both children were asleep in the evenings I was wiped out and had no desire to go anywhere. Being able to take her with me made it possible for me to learn Dutch. Otherwise I would have had to wait until she started preschool and then hope I could find a lesson that fitted into the times where she was away.

The important thing when starting out learning any language is that a little effort goes a long way. Most people will appreciate your efforts to speak their language, especially if they perceive it to be a difficult language and one that few people learn. Be brave and try it out. If you get stuck you can always switch back to English or another language, or ask them to slow down or to explain what a word means if you need to.

Any mistakes are learning moments, so don't fear them. If you wait to speak until you are perfect then you'll never start.

Permanent residency and nationality

Any discussion of gaining permanent residence or nationality depends on the combination of countries involved and your personal details. Where you have come from, what nationality you have, what right you have it by, where you have moved to, how long you've been there for, what your link to the country is (eg married to a national or other ties), and under what rights you are resident.

If you are at all unsure about anything, then you will need to get specialist legal advice from someone who can look at your individual situation and knows the laws in both relevant countries. Below I summarise some things you will need to look into but it is not legally authoritative or anything. This is purely a jumping off point for you to research further.

Most applications for residence or nationality require you to have been temporarily resident legally in that country for a certain length of time. This is another reason it's important for you to register officially when you arrive so that the clock starts on this.

You may also have to pass a certain proficiency in the language and/or understanding of the country's history and culture. There will almost certainly be a cost involved; so if you're interested in this check out the rules for where you're living and talk to other people who have done it.

If you can apply for nationality, then check out the rules for dual nationality - both for your current nationality and the one you're applying for - as you may not be able to have both. Also look at what that would mean for your partner and children.

There can also be special rules for children. Some countries give you the right to nationality if you're born there (though few Western countries do this anymore). And some, like the Netherlands give you the right to choose to become Dutch (instead of anything else) if you spend all your school years resident in the country. So, in 11 or 13 years respectively, assuming the rules don't change, our children will be able to choose to be Dutch or British.

Giving up your previous nationality is a big step and not one to take lightly. But that doesn't mean that it's the wrong decision. And gaining the nationality can have other benefits, like the ability to vote in general elections, or it may become easier to get visas to travel to other countries.

Holding certain nationalities may also require you to fulfil certain obligations, for example, mandatory national service. These are things to investigate and think deeply about before deciding.

Voting

Voting is a big issue, and there are different things you will be able vote on, both where you live and where you're from. If you're registered with the town hall, or police, as a resident then you're probably also on the electoral register and so will receive whatever voting slips you're eligible for automatically. Check if you're uncertain.

Voting in a different place can be disconcerting. The political system and how the number of votes are then allocated towards seats can be very different. The array of political parties will be different, where you have to go to cast your vote will be different and what you're voting for will all be different.

Here in the Netherlands there are general elections, EU elections, local council elections, waterboard elections, and probably more. As EU citizens living here we are entitled to vote in all the local elections, and EU elections (as long as we don't also vote back in the UK), but without a Dutch passport we cannot vote in general elections or in referendums.

We are also still entitled to vote in the UK for general elections, referendums and EU elections (as long as we don't also vote here), but only for fifteen years after we were last resident in the UK. After that date we will have no right to representation there anymore.

Every country treats their expat members differently, so look into what the rules are for your situation. Be aware that depending on the postal service to where you now live you may not be able to receive and return any postal votes before the cut-off date for them to be counted. In which case you can use a proxy vote - where you give someone else resident there the permission to vote on your behalf. You will need to choose someone you trust to vote the way you want them to.

Children leaving home

The decision about where your child will live when they leave home, whether this is to go to University or start work, is one for them to make with your support. Be prepared that they may decide to move back to your home country, which is more likely if they were older when you moved. Or in fact they may decide to move somewhere else entirely. You have given them the exploring bug and now they're off!

Again this depends on how old your children were when you moved and how long you've been there. Do they feel rooted in the community? Where do they feel home is? Do they want to go and explore somewhere else in the same way that you did?

You will need to look into whether your child has the right to home student university fees in either the home country or adopted country. Similarly, will they have the right to work in either country? How do their end of school qualifications compare to the entry requirements for what they want to do?

Comparing university systems in different countries is not always straightforward. You should look at the level of study in an undergraduate course, whether most students live at home or in student accommodation, whether the course is theoretical or applied, and how long the course is for.

There is no right answer to this. Whatever they do and wherever they go will be emotional for you. If they do move away from where you've settled then you know that you've given them a good role model for what is possible. And they're giving you a great excuse to continue your exploring by visiting them where they now live.

Retirement

Lastly, if you're thinking about a permanent move, then you must consider whether or not you plan to retire there. The rules for this vary considerably, so I will only give you questions here, and pointers for what to look for as I can't summarise so well over so many variables.

You may have a right to social pension from your previous place of residence, and you may accrue rights to social pension rights when you become resident in your new country. You may also have multiple employer pensions from different employers, and even a private pension or other investments for your retirement. Whether these can be combined, or have restrictions on what currency they are paid in, and how that is calculated are things you will need to find out.

As you approach retirement age, or plan for it, it would be wise to sit down with a financial adviser who specialises in international pensions and discuss what money you have where and how you might be able to consolidate it. Obviously, when drawing pensions from different countries, there will be implications from the changing currency exchange rates. Different pensions will have different rules about when and how you can draw them, too. Do they give you a lump sum, for you to invest somewhere, or do they give you a monthly pay-out, or a combination of the two?

As a couple you will need to look at all your options for both of you and all pensions you both have. Issues like what payout there is for the surviving partner when one of you dies, and whether any remaining amount is inheritable by your heirs, are points you will need to discuss when choosing the best option for your personal circumstances.

Deciding to move back to your home country can be more difficult than you might expect. You will have had such a different experience, living abroad, to what most of your compatriots have experienced that it might be difficult to just slot back in where you were before. And having lived abroad you will probably look at things in a different way. It can be as much, if not more, of a culture shock moving back as it was to leave.

Thoughts of retirement lead onto those of wills and inheritance. If you have assets in multiple countries, then you will need legal advice on how those assets are likely to be passed on after your death. Some countries have rules about how, and to who, your estate will be split, and deciding which country's laws have jurisdiction can be tricky.

Formalising your last wishes in a will is an important thing to do, to provide you with the surety you know how your loved ones will be looked after if the worst were to happen. You may also be able to appoint a nominated guardian for your children if the situation arises where that is necessary. Be sure you have their agreement before you do this.

There is no one right answer for everyone and only you know what's right for you to do.

Final thoughts

In conclusion, I hope that this book has helped you think through some important things relevant to moving abroad with children. Moving abroad is in itself a big step, and when you add children into the mix, there are even more things to think about and organise. For us, living in a different culture is an eye-opening experience and adds so much value to our lives. I feel truly blessed to have moved and be living abroad and I wish you all the best on your adventure.

I love watching my children develop and learn from both our home background and the community we live in. They are truly getting the best of both worlds. The gift of bilingualism and empathy with multiple cultures will come into its own as they grow and begin their own lives. Whatever they choose to do in the future they will have had this amazing experience growing up.

Moving abroad is a difficult, lonely, journey, but there are others out there who are doing the same. Find them, support each other and it gets a lot easier.

Three things I want to emphasise:

1. What it's like at the beginning isn't how it will stay. Things change and improve. You will get to know people. It will start to feel like home.

2. Just because something is different doesn't mean that it's not as good.

3. Look after yourself.

If you are interested in reading more about our experiences living abroad, then I have another book called "Raising bilingual children: when school speaks a different language". It should be available from the same retailers as this one.

Please find me on social media and tell me all about your experiences moving abroad with your family.

Twitter @clarileia

Instagram @clarissahgosling

Facebook @clarissagosling

I look forward to hearing all about your adventures!

Note from the author

Thank you so much for reading this book. It has been a labour of love and I hope that it has helped you in your adventures moving abroad with your family.

A huge thank you to my husband and children, without you there wouldn't be the basis for this book. You have been so incredibly supportive in my efforts to write and publish this. I couldn't have done it without you. You're the best!

Thank you also to Jonas for the beautiful covers and to Nathalie, Mary, Carole, and Jess for reading an early version of this and giving me comments on it. You made this such a better book.

Check out my website clarissagosling.com[1] to find out what else I've written and what we're up to in our expat adventures!

---

1. http://clarissagosling.com

Copyright

Copyright © 2019 Clarissa Gosling

All rights reserved. This book or any portion thereof may not be reproduced or used in any manner whatsoever without the express written permission of the publisher, except for the use of brief quotations in a book review.

For information, address the publisher at:

info@prinsenhofpublications.com

Clarissa Gosling, Prinsenhof Publications, Box C0274, Keurenplein 41, 1069CD Amsterdam, Nederland

Visit the author's website at https://clarissagosling.com

About the Author

Clarissa has degrees in problem solving and managing information, both of which she uses as best as she can in her writing. She now lives in The Netherlands with her family, where she writes as much as they will let her. She enjoys the puzzle of creating a new world and tying up all the details into a story. You can find out what else she is working on and contact her through her website

Read more at clarissagosling.com.

Made in the USA
Columbia, SC
10 February 2025